Whose Body

Whose Body

Poems
by

Donald Levering

To Gordon Judy,
with love,
Donald
October
2007

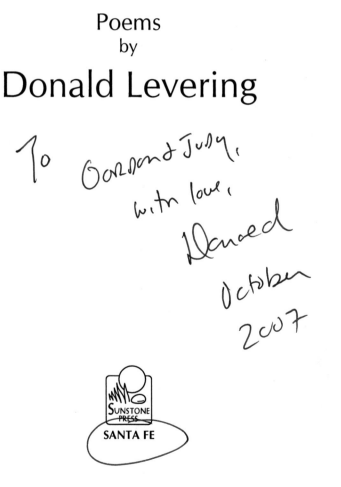

SUNSTONE
PRESS
SANTA FE

Sunstone books may be purchased for educational, business, or sales promotional
use. For information please write: Special Markets Department, Sunstone Press,
P.O. Box 2321, Santa Fe, New Mexico 87504-2321.

Library of Congress Cataloging-in-Publication Data

Levering, Donald, 1949-
  Whose body : poems / by Donald Levering.
    p. cm.
  ISBN 978-0-86534-609-3 (softcovers : alk. paper)
  I. Title.

PS3562.E874W47 2008
811'.54–dc22

                              2007038869

Published in

WWW.SUNSTONEPRESS.COM
SUNSTONE PRESS / POST OFFICE BOX 2321 / SANTA FE, NM 87504-2321 /USA
(505) 988-4418 / ORDERS ONLY (800) 243-5644 / FAX (505) 988-1025

For Camas and Nathaniel

Contents

Acknowledgments

The author is grateful to the editors of the following publications, in which these poems, often in earlier versions, previously appeared:

Anthology, "Dry Spring"
Birmingham Poetry Review, "Get Me God's Name"
Central Avenue, "Missing Thumb," "Two People Touch," "Who Will Come," "Whose Body," "Winter in My Knee"
Commonweal, "Dusk," "Necropolis at Hierapolis"
Desert Shovel, "Cancer"
Fugue, "Spider"
Harwood Anthology, "Her Yuletide Blues"
The Harwood Review, "Humming," "Kayaköy"
The Louisville Review, "On the Back Road to Your Place"
Lunarosity, "Gratitude," "Hats & Shoes," "Previous Lives," "Rooster," "Scuffed Shoe," "To His Diary On Women," "Veiled Love," "Why Not"
The Mid-America Review, "Waking After Independence Day"
Northeast, "Crack in the Sky"
The Pedestal, "Boy—Reprise"
Pemmican, "Why Is The Body Politic"
Rockhurst Review, "Needle of Nothing"
Sin Fronteras: Writers Without Borders, "Astrologer Waiting For A Train," "Musing on a Line from Czesław Miłosz"

Grateful acknowledgment is due to Mary Cost, Sheila Cowing, Melissa Duran, Henry Finney, Richard Lehnert, David Markwardt, Joan Mitchell, Robert Ricci, and Barbara Rockman for their insight on several of the poems. Poems by the poets noted below precipitated or influenced these poems in *Whose Body*:

Cyrus Cassells, "Boy—Reprise"
Po Chü-i, "My Bad Twin"
Edvard Kocbek, "The Bishop's Ring," "Who Will Come"
Joan Mitchell, "The Passion"
Ana Swir, "Why Not"
Arthur Sze, "Needle of Nothing"
Victoria Edwards Tester, "My Star Chart On Audio Tape," "To Ann"
Chuang Tzu, "Boy—Reprise," "Needle of Nothing," "Scuffed Shoe," "Why Not"

Preface

Being written after the work is completed, the preface is only true to its name in that it is that face that appears to the reader before the faces, the mouths, the ears and eyes, and the tails of the poems. The reader may expect that it address where the work came from, what is beneath the surface stratum of words on the pages. So in a sense writing a preface is like trying to answer the Zen conundrum "What are the faces of your original parents?," that sends one whirling backward from present face and circumstances through the ages to those first progenitors. It is a chicken-and-egg proposition that ultimately pulls one into the primal sea asking of one celled organisms, "and who were your parents?" That is to say, these poems came from way before this congregation of flesh & synapses known under my name and their titles.

Whose Body is replete with questions, fifty-nine question marks in the text, to be exact, with other inquiries implied. The title, for example, suggests the question, whose body is this that I occupy, whose body is this that feels love or pleasure or suffers so self-importantly? The infant heard sobbing next door or the tortured political prisoner, are their bodies' aches also not mine? But each is comprised of a certain combination of DNA, so are my body and my self really unique? Another side of the question is, "who is this 'I' that occupies a certain body at a certain time?" Does it maintain an identify apart from the body it inhabits, this body with its specific scars, warm places, habits, and infirmities? Who is this "I" whose memories lightning can replace with healing powers?

I owe much to those who have more masterfully asked these questions before. The early Taoist text of Chuang Tzu provokes these and other questions by use of paradox, pun, exaggeration, and humor. I attempted those devices in this book. One poem opens with a proposition adopted from Chuang Tzu, "Why not turn my arm into a rooster/so it can watch for the false dawn?" Why not wake up to the rooster aspect of yourself, but in doing so, be wary of crowing pseudo-truths. A contemporary mentor of the inciting and insightful question, Czesław Miłosz, uses an open-ended "if" clause to inquire about mortality, "*Oh, if there were one seed without rust inside me.*" Wheelbarrows of speculation depend upon that "if." Other posers of questions in whose wakes these poems follow include another early Taoist, Po Chü-i, the Jewish mystic Moses Maimonides, the Yeats scholar Daniel Albright, and that paragon of propositioners, Jorge Luis Borges. Poets whose lines stimulated specific poems are listed in the Acknowledgments.

In the ancient Chinese texts, puns may be intrinsic to the calligraphic characters, which in one poem raises the question, "What is the character for man/...for woman?" The poetry in two of the sections ponders the relationships between men and women, sometimes in the voice of bewilderment, often in the mode of longing, sometimes in the throes of love and fulfillment, those moments when one's body and intuition are united with another's.

A poet may latch on to an idea and worry it like a dog with a splinter in its paw. One recurring notion in this work is that our very muscles and nerves hold memories. Some forms of therapy aim to heal traumas by unlocking disturbing memories retained in the tissues. Amputees wrestle with ghost sensations in missing limbs, a detached thumb has its memory of love letters it once wrote, a practiced trapeze artist catches

12

hands with a partner mid-air without "thinking"in the head about how it is done.

Another absorption exercised in this book concerns the fabrics that cover our bodies—how a pair of shoes says so much (they have tongues, after all) about its owner, how a hat becomes imbued with the sweat and therefore the DNA of its wearer, or the orgy of guests' coats left to themselves on a bed during a party. Identity gets raised to higher powers of social notice when one's name is emblazoned on a professional sports jersey or a convict jumpsuit.

Practitioners of so-called alternate religious and healing pursuits have influenced the citizenry's beliefs about bodies and souls. One prevalent concept adapted from Hinduism and Buddhism is that of "previous lives," sometimes manifest as the certainty that one can know a specific precursor of one's soul, and can even be "in touch with it" through various ministrations and inducements. Some of these poems contemplate the possibilities of a world where present day selves stand cheek by jowl with their predecessors. Similarly, other identities mirrored here include that of the Doppelgänger and the Bad Twin.

Instead of supplying answers, in this poetry I have striven to give flesh and body to the "dark enigmas" Taoists speak of. Bodies bloom and mutate, lovers cleave and vacillate, dualities of flesh and spirit are created by their very denial. Writing these poems, I imagined a strict Master in the Zen lineage looking over my shoulder ready to whap this body with a stick if a poem started to fall asleep. Or, as Chuang Tzu suggests, behind me all the while was it a butterfly, dreaming me in this body writing poems?

—Santa Fe, 2007

Adept Cart said, "It's amazing! The Maker-of-Things is crumpling me up into such an embrace: a crooked hump sticking out of my back, vital organs bulging over, chin tucked into my belly, shoulders topping skull, nape pointed at sky. And my *ch'i*—its *yin* and *yang* seem all out of whack." Still, his mind remained calm and unconcerned. He hobbled over to the well, looked at himself in the water, and said, "It's incredible! The Maker-of-Things just keeps crumpling me up into this embrace!

—*Chuang Tzu*, translated by David Hinton

I

Whose Body

We tip the body in its coffin
so the juices of decomposition
pour off. Whose body? The robber's

I shot in the gut in the cellar, or one
of the bleeding hermaphrodites
screaming *Dial Nine*

One One? Into which dream did this body
go, the one where I'm floating over Gaudí's
spires in a balloon over Barcelona,

or me made of helium skimming over
treetops, flying right through the trees,
harmless to branches and me?

        ◆   ◆   ◆

In the script burned in the hide
of the bear, my naked body rides
in a cattle car to the masked ball

because I am God's chattel.
Inside, my children maneuver the levers
that bend my limbs backward in awkward

dance. Whose body this that cut its palm
on a broken beer bottle, the scar a flaw
in my life-line, whose fingerprints no less

than galaxy-whorls? Body of the confessed
dreamer, nude to the tongue,
unmasked, undone.

Reunion

You see me as a bearded Sufi
whirling alone with my God
and you reach out to reclaim me

and God how you shake my body
such a shaking as of Saint Vitus
But what's happened to you

lithe lover of old
Your torso has gone El Greco
arms as long as an ape's

and your face in the staccato strobe
is so gaunt
skin stretched like scar tissue from a car wreck

Who was it that night who died
in my car parked in the graveyard
when we wrapped ourselves in our arms

Now your body feels uneasy
When my fingertips brush your angular hips
you hiss in my ear

replacement surgery
And those arms of yours
suffocating as a shroud

Who was it that night who cried out
Since we've reunited
my pelvis has become desire's

cracked bongo
and me but a rattle bones
shuffling across the floor

Crack in the Sky

I saw the crack in the sky
and the lightning-struck tree
into whose hollows, the sunken
cheeks of martyrs, are placed pleas—
Don't let this body get bitten
by the centipede, don't make it
give up its routines.
Oh barkless white saint of an oak,
no surprises please.
I saw the streaks of lightning
at the roots of my lover's hair.

Astrologer Waiting for a Train

for Kathleen Burt

Just me and the galaxy of fruit flies in the basement
when I came to remembering the dream
> *where my horse fell and rolled over me*
> *breaking every bone*
and I woke with my face frozen on one side

The last I remember was the vinegar smell
and the net of fruit flies
turning blackberry sugar to sluggish flight
> *then the horse groaning*
and my cries funneled through half of my face

My lover has turned from my grimace kisses

Can this half moon of a face
be trusted to speak the future
Me with the smirk for a smile
Star struck soothsayer alone in a depot

And when I tripped on the cobblestone
and fell beside the old well
again the dream replayed
> *with the groaning horse rolling over me*
> *cracking my bones*

And I remembered coming to in the basement
inside the knitting of fruit flies
my face gone Picasso

Once with confidence I read the stars
Once my smile was pleasing to myself
Now a chartless star has seized
one side of my face
at the station where strangers

keep looking away

Dusk

The motion sensors switch on floodlights
as I walk past the houses of the rich
Here I was so righteous
walking for my heart in the cold
But the sensors know the darkness
I carry within me
I want to cry out *I am not covetous*
I don't have cancer
My thoughts are no worse than the next man's
but another lamp flares as I pass

Her Yuletide Blues

The spruce's tiny blue lights
poke holes in the sky
draining all color but blue
She ruminates on the man
who traded his brewery for a tulip

She looks long at her hands

Her room inside so full of darkness
Full of pipes like a brewery's copper tubing
Pipes clogged with the thought
of a blue tulip bought for a brewery
If only she could move

In her dream where souls are pilot lights in a cellar
she keeps bumping into the brewer
and the brewer demands
What will you do with your shackles removed?
Where will you place your hands?

Wakes with her heart in her throat
Mulls over the story
Tells it to herself again and again
The story of the man who traded
his brewery for a blue tulip

If only her father

It was a virus she says to herself
A virus that made this tulip
unfold in blue flames
A virus that made it mutate
If only the brewer would stop prying

She goes over the story
There was a man who freed himself
of bushels of hops and barley boilers
A man no longer cramped by copper tubing
Man who abandoned his family

All for a blue tulip

If only the tree lights would stop blinking
If only the spruce weren't tricked in blues
If only the holly leaves weren't so sharp
If only the fluid would drain
If only she could reach the surface

She puts on music
If only Billie Holiday didn't croon so sadly
If only she weren't so black and blue
If only Billie's vowels didn't leak from her marrow
If only her songs didn't drain so slowly

If only her own hands

If the only story were of the tulip bulb
dormant under snow
If only she could breathe
If only her story were a white canvas
If only her father loved her less

If only his hands hadn't

Can't stop bumping into the brewer
Can't stop thinking
Brewery for a tulip
Tulip bartered for a brewery
If only the sky weren't poked so full of holes

Cancer

*...designs multiply dizzyingly, dizzyingly
mutate into other designs,
with something of the disturbing
abundance of nature itself...*
                    —Daniel Albright

My friend who spawns strong women
characters in her fiction,
she with the hole in her esophagus,
writes to tell me her cancer
is not as ravenous as others'.
She's improved, after all,
from feeding tubes to spooning broth.
She feels luckier than my neighbor
Paul, who once painted colors
even mutating tulips couldn't produce,
whose lungs are riddled with spots.
He marks the days of his sentence
married to a breathing machine.

Some cancers hole up
in obscure corners of the body,
like homeless men curled harmlessly
under stairwells. Others go and come
like salesmen leaving calling cards.
Sometimes a liver or pancreas
will read them into their cells
and then the sale's complete, body gone
down the staircase to hell. Hell
of hauling a body of pain
bigger than the body, larger
than the fame of the Beatle

too weak to pick up a guitar pick,
burning on the bank of his Ganges.
Ganja may have eased the pain,
along with his *Rastaman Vibration,*
but couldn't stop the cancer
seeding like a pomegranate
in the father of reggae's brain.
And I remember John Hartford's lively body
wholly given over to music,
at once clogging, fiddling,
and singing a song.
Shortly before leukemia stilled him,
he appeared in a movie, hoarse wraith
with gallows' humor.

Nature's design in this misery,
it seems, is to keep transmuting,
like arabesques in Persian tapestries,
fantastic beasts in the *Book of Kells*
sprouting body parts, arpeggios
rolling from throats and off fingertips,
life and art a riot
of self-engendered change.
Would I spare some for the beggar
crouched under the stairwell,
neck distended with lymphoma,
or spend it on a bootleg disc of Dolphy,
whose forehead's bulbous tumor
morphed dolphin trills and squeaks
into music from his horn,   ⇨

bellows from Picasso's minotaur,
minor chords from the painter's blue guitar,
the twentieth century embodied
in replicating cubes of skyscrapers,
cloned sheep, Franco
as polyp-monster, Picasso
drawing satyrs in gardens,
sculpting goats from flowerpots,
painting pendulous breasted
pregnant women, saying
Every artist is a woman,
frisky as his pet monkey
till he died at ninety-one
cancer free.

Missing Thumb

Thumb in the hospital dumpster.
Its owner fumbles with its ghost.
It has its story, the screws

turned, fishing flies tied,
compass points guided.
Or maybe in its muscle memory

stitching quilts, braiding hair,
cinnamon pinches sprinkled on dough.
Whatever it has picked up

to bring to the nose
or turn before the eye
is missing only when memory goes.

The five aces spread in a fan,
the songs picked on a banjo
today can only be played

inside the brain.
Recall the cursive trail
of new words being learned,

of love letters. But now—
the new way of writing
without a thumb.

Scuffed Shoe

Scuffed toe of your shoe, mark
of drop foot, of arteries
clogged in your brain.
Your body isn't fooled
by shining your shoe—
beneath your calluses are scored
the miles you've galloped
toward an end unseen,
known by the body
for what it is.
So your foot drags
as the great wind before you
scours everything in its path—
the forest with its howling
hollows, stars streaking
through their courses, the runaway
horse, the aging traveler
with the wise body
dragging its foot.

Ringing Ears

That high pitched noise I try to ignore
as the mind behind-the-scenes
flips through its index—modem,
tea kettle, bus transmission—
and passes on to mind-of-fear—
dentist's drill, missile, torture tool—
and finally files under ringing ears,
and then goes on for cause—
one too many pain pills,
or last night's synthesizer
wailing the musician's outrage
at what is wrong with the world
and his clinging to what is dear.

Perhaps the overtones
of last month's temple gong
are going on in the background
with the call to quietude,
to listen to this body telling me
what?—that restlessness rings
through my marrow, that the world
deserves a permanent alert,
that I need to be lashed
to my ship of resolution
to keep from succumbing to sirens.
My teacher invites me to sit
and listen to the mind's
tintinnabulation, to what is
behind the noise of my life,
to observe the expectation
that there be silence
as the world screeches through travesty
and catastrophe,
to recognize the desire
for calm
in the face of what is.

Kidney Stones

The evolutionary process culminates in the convergence
of the material and the spiritual into a superconsciousness.
—Pierre Teilhard de Chardin

Through white-hot pain he hears
the tinkle of kidney stones in the bowl
and when the avalanche has passed
sweat beads on his brow
sleet ticks against the window

And all his agony
all the suffering ever caused others
is crystalized
along with all the bliss
just as the sugars and salts on his tongue
had been converted to kisses and curses

Regrets like the spurs of kidney stones
passing through his urethra

And it occurs to him
if he had never offended
never had given of himself
he would never have passed
through the gates of pain and pleasure
he'd be no more
than a brain with its body

His daughter brings him
cranberry tea for his kidneys
sweetened with honey

He asks himself
what is his soul
but an aggregate of mind and body

What is mind but a cocklebur husk
around the body
as it passes through the world

This is the pain he thinks
a man must navigate
to attain the body's
vigor and grace

Bodies interlocking
in the chain of DNA
spiraling from cells in the primal sea
to plankton to spiny urchins
on and on through to his
daughter
or honeybees

The body fast on the trail to its death
the instant of conception

So where is soul inserted
in the muscle memory
of the trapeze artist
tumbling through air

Where in the world is unloosed
Chardin's *noosphere*
that net of neurons firing
from impulse to reason
to thoughts of God and soul

⇨

In that instant of crystalized ache
as the stones pass
he feels an inkling
of the pain of childbirth
his mother suffered
he sees how his thoughts
harden into words
about the world
not the world
but the words of the world

He smiles at the thought
of the *Oxford English Dictionary*
tumbling through his urethra

Smiling at his daughter
he puts his tongue
on the lip of the honey jar
to get the grit in his teeth
of honey crystals

Where would the pain be sharper
Where would it be sweeter
than this ticking of sleet on his window

—for John Lofflin

II

Rooster

Before the turbines begin to turn,
a rooster is crowing
in the belly of a 747—

Screw You! Screw You!

His outrage offers levity
to passengers shuffling to their seats.

Through taxi and liftoff
he crows and crows
as the co-pilot palms the flap controls.

♦   ♦   ♦

The jet dips a wing to the harbor.
Mortals below blink at its glint of windows.
It seems a single shining purpose
as the babel of tongues within
is concealed by its thunder.

♦   ♦   ♦

In 17C a woman won't let go
of her gravity.
She sneaks a cell-phone call,
Did you remember
to turn off the coffeepot?
In his cage The Cock God
flaps and crows—

Cock-a-doodle-doo!

as the plane bores deeper
into 14F's novel
whose characters are ruled
by stars of self-delusion.   ⇨

◆　　◆　　◆

Through a tiny slit by a rivet
the rooster's red eye sees
barnyards shrinking.
Time zones pass through the bird
still crowing
as a few on board begin to snooze.

◆　　◆　　◆

A newspaper read over a shoulder
quotes another flight's cockpit recorder—
Allah hu Akbar—
My fate is in your hands,
as the co-pilot pulled the flaps down
and a boatload of plans
screamed into the blue.

◆　　◆　　◆

The rooster keeps crowing
unheard by the lady in 37A
channeling a prophet from Sirius,
who asserts our fates are self-created.
                              Untrue! Untrue!

In her seatmate's earphones
Mississippi John Hurt croons
"Rich woman knows
any dude'll do."

◆　　◆　　◆

The newspaper reader's eyes close.
Black & white afterimages
recreate the scene
of an Airbus of fates

plummeting in a vortex
of screams heart attacks
prayers clenched jaws
plunging into water breaking
the jetliner's spine
into a million descents,
soaked baggage of past & future lives
raining to the sea floor.

        ♦   ♦   ♦

The fowl on high
continues crowing
as the Boeing breaks through the ceiling
and rises above the white buffalo cumulus
where dwell the souls of 19th Century
American landscape painters
beyond the plains of manifest destiny.
Delusions! Delusions!

My Bad Twin

           climbs into bed
with the woman who's convinced
her life as an Incan princess
made more sense than this one.

At least it's more real, he says
like he gives a shit, but her eyes
don't quite track, and neither knows
on what level they're lying.

She keeps mistaking me for him,
who has farted, left the bed,
poured himself another drink,
left the lights on, and packed another pipe

of hallucinations more interesting
than this addled dame from another life.
The righteous thing for him to do
is to summon the Zen marines,

who shave her head
and force feed her koans
so that the Dark Enigma
might be revealed within.

After much prodding, she still
doesn't quite get it,
so the Buddhist brownshirts
assign her ten thousand Poundian cantos

and canter away on horses
my bad twin has fed foxglove
to make them shine like prizefighters
before their hearts give out.

He shrugs at the horses' luck,
at the meaning of his lover's previous lives,
says, *What the fuck?*,
and does nothing.

Why Not

Why not turn my arm into a rooster
so it can watch for the false dawn?
This sore finger could flute
the falling leaves of cottonwoods.
The carapace I've grown to keep away pain,
why not drill it full of holes for divination?
My sloughed skin could be formed
into the Great Clod of Agriculture,
spittle into the web
of the Master of Eight Legs.
Tumor of anger in my chest,
with it club the liar President.
As for my buttocks, large
with fake prosperity,
make them tractor wheels,
that I might roll my body
to the house of Carnal Knowledge,
might roll my body to the charnel house.
Might light it with a burst of laughter.

Newfoundland

The words remained with him after he woke
with his penis engorged,
You no longer need the two frog bodies.
Certain he would leave behind with his wife
his name and his twin frog-nesses,
he would walk away
from his Iowa belongings
and migrate to a fish-house off Newfoundland.
How eager he was to call himself
whatever he pleased, to jettison
his parents' mores.
How grateful to relinquish the tool
of his father's lust
and not to assume
his mother's dutiful looks.
Swollen burdens no more,
no more concatenated surnames,
relief from worry over mortgage and spawn.
Simply circling dark blue icebergs
with his shimmering school of new companions,
or blissfully being blown off course,
waking with but a single name
and just one body to thread through the sea.

Waking After Independence Day

Can I be sure it was a dream,
or did an alien really plant
in my brain the Molecule
of Purification? Might it be
that the woman I'm trying to woo
finally turned her head?
Are the spent starburst shells a clue,
or just the refuse of another
revolution around the sun?
The snake that molted beneath my tree,
what would it whisper about
this pomegranate I found
when I awoke? Inside,
a million seeds.

Gratitude

grows out of the left side of my torso.
        The young nun glimpsed it
        just as the wind
                lifted her habit.
        The bigot couldn't get his gloves
                        around it.

        The bee took a strand
                and circled my home,
        once for the hive,
                once for the honey of heather.

        What if I gave it to you?
        You might take it for the glimmer
                of the eel in the well
                        or the twang of the banjo.

        Feeling the way I do,
        you might include the twinge of tendinitis
                that proves you're not a shadow.

Protruding from your heart,
        would it embarrass you?
                You might give it to another.

Spider

To make a joyful sound,
just let the divine spider
climb out of your mouth
and go about its business
tying knots around your life.
So you're a marionette,
you still can feel yourself dancing
no matter who's pulling the strings.
Even as your divorce decree
is signed, the spider
goes on marrying you
to corners of household dust.
Eight legs, a ravenous mouth,
and the yen to spin silk in shadows.
Who wouldn't sing?

Humming

Between the painful bite of the centipede
and the whir of the Rufous' wings
his head was humming.
And if the ringing outlives him
his curve-ball fingers will turn
into a tuning fork, his vertebrae
become pebbles in a streambed.

While he was sleeping the snake
molted under the tree
and he awoke aroused and weeping.
Now he could feel
that every spine was sending him signals,
now he received all frequencies.

Invitation

The countless spines
beckon mine to align.
To bow toward the Mecca
of Earth's magnetism
and bend with bamboo in the wind.
To quit knuckling under to cynicism
and turn my aching sacrum
into compassion's dowsing stick.
The giraffe's 97th vertebra
has me humming B natural
octaves above melancholia.
Standing tall as the masts of sailing ships
I am called to dive in the sea
and curve my body into a strand
of the annual eel migration.
To feel the surge from the Earth's core
up my spine, my dendrites
filaments of the northern lights.

Get Me God's Name

Not just the consonants in clattering hailstones

Not only the letters disguised as numbers
that can never be sung

but the Word incarnate
tsunami of sound splintering bone houses

Not just the code for cloning lost sheep

but the infrared sirens of orchids
the vowels of birth and mourning

Then name the face before the first face
Count the gnats out of whose humming
hatches the singing seraphim

Call out the world before original sin
Absolve all guilt
before the deeds are done

Now answer my doubts with a passage
played on the sad violin

Christen the father of serpents
who left me this shed skin

Tell if the tension in my hand
as it struck the gong
caused Mr. Wen to pluck the wrong lute string

Stir the susurrus of the first forest wind
Replay the cries of the earliest orangutan

Reveal the faces of our original parents
in the grain of the glad violin

Musing on a Line from Czesław Miłosz

Oh, if there were one seed without rust inside me

If there were a thought constructed of pure thought
instead of electricity
If the cadaver did not twitch

One spore within
that never relinquished
its song of the infinitely small

One muscle that forever maintained its resolve
If one corpuscle of my blood
swam through the flames of cremation

One species removed from the list of extinctions
A single act without a past
One unrenounceable love

Then would I beget
legions of angels
visible to the greatest skeptics

If one neutrino passing through
paused to consider our condition
Then would I exalt our communal lint

If compassion were as ample as motes
Then would I massage my neighbor's feet
Then would I grow young and die blooming

Kayaköy

In the center of the village
inhabited by goats and crows
is the well from the dream
the sister I never had
dug for me with her bare hands.
Beside it a bucket of dust.
Twelve years to murder our brothers,
she complains, and when I wake,
I'm the only son of our father
remaining in this ruined church
with fig trees growing through the floor.
A billy goat chewing on a thistle
eyes me—I see myself in his pupil.
I listen for my brothers' voices
among the church's stones
but all I hear are echoes
of communal prayers.
My sister had sung
for her hands to grow back,
her singing so pure
it still hurts.
Oh where are my brothers?

Necropolis of Hierapolis

Sickly rich Romans once flocked
to the healing spring close by.
Those that lost reside on this ridge
covered with hundreds of tombs
with a view of the shimmering wheat fields.
Into one cool chamber climb my son and I—
it smells of must that coats my lungs.
We stay in the darkness a quiet moment,
then he clambers out
and bounds to the circular sepulcher
with the proud phallus on top.
But I remain inside
with the specter of his mother
breathing hard.

Who Will Come

Loneliness like a rain soaked flag,
longing in the loins,
who will come to me this morning?
My dreaming's more draining than toiling,
my cravings clangorous as the F-Train.
What to do with this self-pity,
this body no longer young,
its sore back, the fist
with its missing thumb?
Memory is a maudlin drunk,
his flushed face in mine, panhandling.
Could I give him my seventeenth year
with its thumbs up confidence,
the better days of a marriage
now defunct?
Each day the stubble-faced Doppelgänger
I descend with in the mirrored elevator
grows more shabby,
every day I hear him thinking
the same of me.
Who will come to me this morning?

The Bishop's Ring

is inlaid with babies' teeth.
For years I'd been bowing
to kiss it, never quite reaching
it, the whole while hearing behind me
trains coming and going,
drunken wedding entourages,
newspaper hawkers, the cawing
of undertaker crows.

My train departed cathedral station
ages ago, but my car came uncoupled
and rusts on a spur in this echoing depot
where my grown daughter
in dark tuxedo is playing saxophone
for my late-night divorce party.
The emcee holds the pigeon
for me to whisper a wish in its ear.

To His Diary on Women

Why does the moon that rules over women
cloud over
the moment I enter a room?

I'm quick to light candles
and offer my hand for a dance,
but not nimble enough to keep them

from snuffing the flames from their eyes.
It has little to do with comeliness—
worse looking men will kindle the coals

beneath their soft skin.
The guys who win them over
have cracked the code of intimation

girls perfect by second grade.
Don't think I buy "the feminine mystique,"
it sounds like a pitch for mascara.

I never could throw curve balls,
and mascara is a mystery
the Mexican poetess must have been wearing,

the way I couldn't quit staring.
Thin as a hieroglyphic cat,
she was perfectly inscrutable.

My ¡Hola!
may as well have been Cobol.
Then there's the issue of perfume.

Ladybird beetles use pheromones.
I wore a football helmet
and fumbled passes.

Self-Portrait with Pets

In the background his golden retriever
       who ate chunks of asphalt
         and barked at ghosts
           who chewed through his chain
             and swallowed his teeth
               has just knocked over the flower vase

                                    Calico cat
                         in the chair covered in hair
                      whose traces of saliva
              tell her whatever she needs to know
           about herself
         adoze in her chair

Half-Crow astrologer
        lifts off his shoulder
          out the window
            toward two cedars
              in worried weather

                             Fox-colored beard
                   beneath untamed eyebrows

              One pinhole pupil
           the other a black dime

Longings in the form of a pair of rabbits
                  floating à la Chagall
                          beside the nimbus of kindness
              or is it indecision

           The paint cracking as it dries on his face

The Invisible Man Dances with the Stripper

All he could think of was Raskolnikov's saintly prostitute
as she shimmied to the brushes and the high-hat
and strutted with the comical trombone
kicking off her slippers
amidst the shrill whistling

Funny when it came down to it
she didn't have much of a body
having offered pieces to sextillions
But he could see her soul
was as large as Joan of Arc's

as she burned in the spotlight of their fantasies
oblivious to his shuffling nearby
her eyes cast heavenward
lifting one leg to slip her garter off
tossing it with her implicit promises

His face invisibly blazed
with shame for her
whose teasing was multiplied in mirrors
taking off her negligee
and then her bra to the catcalls

When she dropped her G-string
he'd never felt so nude
to see her shaved bare as a baby
Never had he longed harder
for a body that could cover hers

Wanting It

I covet my neighbor's wife.
Such lovely green eyes
that rarely go into mine.
And my other neighbor, her breasts,
her fierce feminism.
I crave Paula's long legs,
love her blocky Picasso feet.
Annette's husky voice,
Tracy shaking me in a heat.
I envy Joyce's delicate hands
and Carol's sweet soprano.
Francine's sibilant speech,
her curvaceous ways
to get her way.
How Blanche makes statements
in the form of questions.
The wide hips for child bearing,
how women make conversation
like endless weaving.
The dashes in Emily Dickinson—
Sappho's unabashed desire.
I want to penetrate them all—
I want them all inside me.

Needle of Nothing

What is the character for *man*?
For this one, no different from *tree*—
arms diminished to dry limbs

embracing nothing but wind.
This tree has been waiting
for the calligrapher

to change it back to a man.
Waiting, feeling nothing
but the weight of a locust lighting.

The writer arrives
to turn himself into a needle
of nothing,

for my lover has made of me a twig
lying in the parched creek bed.
Waiting to revive

with the frogs in the next rain.
What is the character for rain?
For *woman*?

Dry Spring

If my eyes are puffy with pollen,
might I miss another entry
in the annals of lust?

If the wind is blowing the dry sticks
of my bones, would my cigarette
eat a hundred prickly acres?

The calendar flips over
on another hot one.
Shaking my pen, sucking it

to force the flow. Spent
prophylactic in the dust
of the arroyo. Longing

in the bottom of the rainbarrel.
A million buds are thirsting
for meaning. I'm tapped out,

but keep repeating
the rain dance done
under a thousand suns.

Keep coming on
with the black tongue
of my heartless seductions.

Keep clearing my throat,
sweeping my entranceway
for one who doesn't come.

The Winter in My Knee

limps me away from the dance floor's
mating arena, where my would-be
lover's lazy eye wanders
from my attentions.
It will not suffer me to kneel
to the crucifix, or genuflect
before the ceramic blue coyote.
It hobbles me with my Burgundy
to the chill window sill
with the inert fly
where I look inside
while my eyes rest on the horizon.

What can be seen but my liver
gone to the Great Beyond,
my tongue being hawked in the market,
along with my volumes of self-pity,
along with the blue potato
of my knee
that fixes my attention here
where it hurts, where I worry it
like a dog's tongue on a splinter.
Or here, where my penis is longing.
And here, where I mind my own business,
mind my own business, heartless.

My Star Chart on Audio Tape

Walked my longing into winter's arroyo.
A place to bury it must be nearing,
but no, I keep going upstream
as the dusk deepens and I stumble
on rocks I can no longer see.

Last week with Buddhists
sitting in stillness.
Tuesday reeling with Sufis.
Into my ears the astrologer speaks
of the instant before birth,

the last gasp of the unencumbered soul,
my moon in the house of Scorpio,
how Neptune could plunge me under
drugs' delirium
but for poetry's counter pull.

What can this mean for these yearnings
impelling me blindly onward?
My Buddha may as well be dwelling
on the other side of the moon
concealed beneath the horizon.

Just before the ruling star
of all our earthly woe and bliss
drops from view, a patch of snow
on the east bank of the arroyo
grows luminous, lit from within.

IV

Why Is the Body Politic

wearing the gloves of abductors,
doesn't it love kisses on fingertips?
Why hooded from your lovely eyes?
Why digging secret graves in the woods
that scintillate with butterflies?

◆   ◆   ◆

In dignified witness
before the Presidential Palace
in Buenos Aires, mothers
in white headscarves
silently pace with placards
displaying the faces and names
of *the disappeared*

◆   ◆   ◆

Whose son's or daughter's cries
are gagged in the next room,
neighbor nation,
whose body but our own
suffers the beating
on the soles of the feet?

◆   ◆   ◆

As the Argentine mothers mutely,
eloquently circle,
thousands of letters arrive in Ankara
demanding the immediate
and unconditional release
of Leyla Zuna
whose "crime" was speaking Kurdish
in the Turkish parliament

⇨

♦   ♦   ♦

Why am I blessed with the warmth
                    of your hand on my thighs
when electrodes are clipped
                    to my brothers' genitals?

♦   ♦   ♦

...mailbags full of letters
to the president of Ethiopia
demanding release
Diribi Demissie
held incognito
in a cell in Addis Ababa.

♦   ♦   ♦

Through our apartment's walls
come the infant's cries for the breast,
                not in the Spanish of its parents,
                    or in my English,
                        or my brother's Turkish,
                but in the diction of suck and sob
                        known to mothers and lovers
                            like you and me
                in want of the nourishment
                        of the caress
                        of fingertips and palms,
                our bodies' crying out with pleasure
as the baby next door coos

♦   ♦   ♦

The mothers continue
their silent procession.
The faces and names that they carry
                    refuse to be erased.

Two People Touch

each other's fears
ravens on a streetlamp sharing some glistening thing

Is it foil that will tear them up inside
or is it some nourishing thing
something they can take deep within
·fuel for the great breast muscles of flight

Some thing that feeds the blast furnaces
of their passion

Something they may be afraid to name
though they could call it love

could call it staving off the darkness
could keep them in the moment from the cold

Two people touch
                              something glistening
between them
                              something aflame

Look at the Lovers

running through the airport
giggling all the way,
a flag of underwear waving
from their suitcase.

It's clear that they've lingered in bed.
Apparent they give not a fig
that children are staring
as they kiss in the queue.

Can you remember
when you were as happy as finches?
Do you blush
re-reading love letters?

Now they have brushed past customs,
now their passports are valentines.
Now they are rushing down the runway,
leaping from their shadow, flying.

The Invisible Man Courts the Dancer

Because she cannot see me,
I'll woo her with my voice
persistent as a cricket, big as the wind.
She'll keep wondering *from where*
are these compliments coming, who
compares me to Cleopatra,
why is he praising my large feet?
What is this whispering in my ear
giving me shivers and more?
And I will speak the lost volumes
from the shelves of love
in the vast library of Alexandria
burning in a hot wind.
If she still cannot feel me near,
I will become the music
she becomes when she dances.

The Shy Man Considers a Quote
from Jay Wright

It is simple to ache in the Bone, or the Rind.
Sit here with me, near this solitude,

where the chamisa's shadow
sounds a minor chord,

reverberates, quivering in wind.
All day the sound sustains

below the bush's yellow blooms
whose cloying scent lures

yellow jackets in autumn sun.
The shadow turns from olive

to maroon as the sun pivots
around the shrub.

Simple to stay rooted
to the bulbous shadows

that ring the hubbub of the day.
To observe, remaining mute

though the heart longs to chime
and the voice struggles for a starting place.

Veiled Love

Could my passion be hidden from her
among the facets of autumn aspen leaves
A love so vast and flaming she cannot grasp it

Perhaps my love is dispersed
among purple cirrus at sunset
Maybe it's lost between stars

She comes to me with outstretched arms
in the dream where starlings gather in swirling gusts
and are gone at dusk

In the wing beats of a pair of cranes
is that her I hear
whispering to another

Matinee

Béla Tarr's "Werckmeister Harmonies"

In this black & white saga
of confused revolution,
the largest whale in the world
has been stuffed like a trophy
and hauled in a mammoth trailer
through darkness to the heart
of a landlocked city.
All night its glass eyes
stare at the trailer's walls

and in the morning the curious
are sold tickets to view.
What is this whale if not my heart
grown old as Methuselah
in a stale marriage,
what could I have foreseen
that wouldn't have been distinct
twenty thousand leagues under the sea
to a lover schooled in his feelings?

The masses are burning bonfires
in the square where the whale presides,
now they invade the hospital
pulling the sick from their beds.
Who is the aged patient they find
naked in the shower
if not me,
staring at upheaval's minions
with fearful eyes?

In this tale of one man's loyalty
and of betrayals,
            who is the author
of the coup d' état of my heart?

The film unfolds in eclipses,
shadows overcoming light in nightsweat streets,
the light once again blossoming at dawn
to reveal the walls around the whale
torn down.

            The man left standing
in the abandoned square
who was blind to the mutiny
until too late, this man with his hands
over his face, the lens,
is he none other than me
leaving the theater holding hands
with loneliness, walking out empty
at twilight into the snow-lit street?

On the Back Road to Your Place

                                the cars kicked up dust in my face
I was mistaken for homeless with my ragged backpack
I was mistaken for heartless with my understatement
I was mistaken
                        before I found the back road
            the unpaved hesitating way
to your place

Before I found the right route
                    One woman teased me
                    Another kept forgetting my name
On other roads I kept making roundabouts
                    I kept to myself
I kept turning back toward my old nest

            On the back road to your place
                        I coughed from the dust of a housewife shaking rugs
                        I crossed a cat in heat
                                    I was cursed by a raven overhead
                        I was trailed by feral dogs
            I was mistaken for my fears

On the back road divorce
            imperfect children imperfect husbands and wives
On the back road detours
                                ruts of regrets
                                        meandering

On the back road I became impatient with the back road
On the back road I wished for the expressway

On the back road I finally opened my hands
I leafed out with the cottonwoods
                    that straddle the way to your place
        I ran through the culvert where lovers' names
                            are knotted in spray paint
                    I kept going I kept going

On the back road you were on the way to my place

To Ann

Last night I stitched my shadow to yours.
It was within Billie Holiday weeping like a wound,
within your honey-colored skin by candlelight.
Within you I felt the stitching start to close

the darkness between stars that is our fear.
We swam in kisses along the full lengths
of our otter bodies bobbing,
breathless, garmentless,

floating the underground stream
beyond our fears of belonging
and abandonment, into the humming
deep inside the cave from where we came,

before original parents, before shame,
before crystal and carbon, deeper
toward the core, our bodies fused and whirling
among the birthing galaxies.

Jupiter's Red Spot

To think that Jupiter's large red spot,
big enough to hold two Earths,
is a never-ending tempest,
mother of all hurricanes
from whence passion comes and returns—
It's enough, by Jove, to make the peaceful
introvert in me want to
pick a fight, dance a tango,
revel unbridled and high.
Caught up in its gassy swirl
are ions enough to light up
every New Year's Eve
and wedding celebration.
Under this ruddy heart of Jupiter,
no truck with Neptune's lugubrious tides
or Pluto's cold stare;
instead, ardent affirmations,
rapid anger, banner-waving fervor,
sprinting after the *umpah umpah*
of the band wagon tubas.
So when I've triggered Ann's temper
and am banished,
I have to go to Jupiter
to get her purple roses,
I need to dive into the cyclone
and bring her back its calm,
unwavering eye.

The Passion

Potato eyes in their wire basket
      see spring coming

    Each eye is growing its pale El Greco body

      Across the street the girls in white dresses
        pose for a photo before the church

The spuds are growing soft inside
    and I am falling in love
      with daffodils peaking through snow
        falling in love with Paula
          and with the evenings' long drinks of light

Bees are weaving their spell
    through apricot blossoms
      on a once bare tree

    But in this season of abstinence
             (counting the days
        before the first Sunday
      after the first full moon
    after Vernal Equinox)
Paula begins wavering

    and things get complicated—
   my daughter's dress stained by first menses
  the vinegar sponge raised on a stick
        to mock the Nazarene's thirst
  the purple lashes on the backs of Penitentes
my love forsaking me

Until the vinegar smell
        of the dyeing of eggs
                crimson as Christ's blood
awakens me
      to Demeter's return from the Underworld
          wearing the white slippers of crocus blooms

Potato eyes wriggling toward light
          each the body of an El Greco crucifixion

And I feel the midday sun
              stirring the worms in the sod
       smell the yellow fur
          inside budding irises

       feel myself turning
              inside out

V

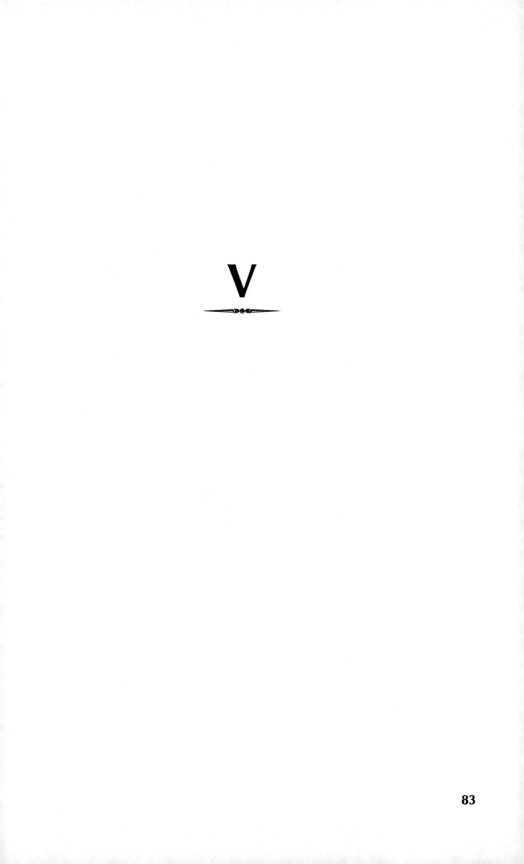

Previous Lives

When things get sticky she tells me
that once we were Indians
who made love in full regalia
so much more spiritually
than our sucking and grinding saying *yes*

don't stop yes Oh Yes.
On the bus a woman waved her hand
to dismiss us—skinny schoolgirl
with impish smile, stubble-faced drifter
smelling of beer, guy with the bike,

matron wearing a pillbox hat, me—
She proclaimed, *None of you were with me*
when I was Queen of England.
There was no denying her.
But when my lover's shaman guided me

through the tunnel of my previous lives,
it was like passing another subway train
on Hallowe'en, and when the rocking
of the ages stopped, the doors opened
on an ordinary Joe in well-worn brogues,

working under a lord for a pittance,
unread, unadorned, wart prone,
yet loving a sad song or a lively dance,
strong ale, a wild and funny story,
aye, and a rollicking roll in the hay.

All of Me

What she wanted was
the song *All of Me* with variations
She wanted me to play it
on the cello of her pelvis
No she wanted to play hardball
What she wanted was to carry me in her suitcase
and plug me in in her hotel room

She wanted *All of Me* played in every key
No she wanted me unchanging
like the cicada shell clamped onto
the utility pole outside her door
She wanted my utility pole
She wanted me to shrill *All of Me*
all the long cicadan August

She wanted me home she wanted me on the road
What she wanted was to exhaust me
She wanted me to play utility infielder
She wanted to keep score of every play
No she wanted my scoreboard organ
to repeat *All of Me* the same way
All she wanted was my long ball song

Bone Fixer

Now you're a good liar
not knowing any better
claiming you were on a vision quest

up on Mule Mesa when it
pierced the metal button
at the crown of your baseball cap

and left you through your thigh
knocked down
by the sound that lingers

Tonight under the big top
begged by the woman
we've seen limping for months

to mend her aching hip
you can't remember your lame story
or where you were really headed

when the brightness
chose you bone fixer for our tribe
the one to cure

this flushed face of the hole
in his windpipe
and of the wine that burned it

to heal this griever's broken ribs
clear the blur from that bitch's eye
ease my shoulder's hurting

⇨

Whoever it was whose memory
was seared that day from your head
opened a space for believers

under a tent as big as sky
for a voice as real as thunder's
to erase their pain

Boy—Reprise

It's true I drowned at six.
True when I was twenty
we lifted above the city

as the sky filled with spy satellites.
No one believed our balloon
could still be afloat
when the moon rose to make of the sea
a threshing floor.
But above it all we glowed
as our burners flared.

We breathed from our heels
in the dear air,
our fingertips kissed from blue to pink.

♦   ♦   ♦

boy that I am I rush into water over my head
to rescue the beach ball
drifting deeper on the tide.
All purpose, scampering over the surface
like a water strider,
I'm closing in on the ball
when I hear the others calling,
fear in their voices
that the boy cannot swim,
and I begin the thrash of drowning.

♦   ♦   ♦

⇨

Beneath us the City of Romance
kept shrinking, obscured by clouds,
each hint as thin as a cicada wing,
but piled as dense as cicada song.
The masses below breathed from their throats
as the sky bristled with hardware.
Who can tell whether the stars
or our fears
punctured our promises?

Hard earth rushed toward our heels.
Falling fast and faster, I recalled
an earlier rescue,

♦   ♦   ♦

fighting the water, strong arms
brought me back to land,
vomiting brine onto sand.

♦   ♦   ♦

Slammed into a slope in the Andes.

I woke to the sound of a gimlet
prying open my jaw
to extract the silver of my years.

Abandoned again, my blood dried
into flakes of iron
scattered in mountain wind.

♦   ♦   ♦

I revived in the unburial
of the sacrificial Incan boy
and his twin sister
mummified at the summit.
King and Queen for a year
before our ritual murder,
we were exhumed to travel
in coffins of dry ice
to museum immortality.

♦   ♦   ♦

I swim over canyons, condors
for kin, my sibling in love
a wingtip away.

National Geographic

Evolution began when simple cells
in the sea developed eyes.

The family tree of terrestrial life
spreads across two pages filled with facts.
Hanging from the primate branch
is a chimpanzee, who uses tools
and wages war, who gives signs
of self-consciousness, whose DNA
is 98 percent the same as humans'.

◆   ◆   ◆

Elizabeth Bishop at six
sits in a dentist's waiting room
paging through a *National Geographic*.
Horrified at the natives' naked breasts,
she stares at their necks ringed like light bulbs.
The stuffy room is full of grown-ups.
To herself she says, "You are an *I*,"
not a Tutsi with terrible breasts,
not one of these grown-ups
she is shy of in this room,
not her foolish aunt,
who just now cries out in pain
from the inner office, but
"an Elizabeth," a separate self.

◆   ◆   ◆

Photos: the walking whale of Pakistan
fossilized in desert sandstone

Our cousin the fruit bat
midwifing another's breech birth

Morning dew on the web
of the sixteen-eyed wolf spider

◆　　◆　　◆

In Sri Lanka the Tiger boy
poses with his carbine.
Does he ever see himself
apart from revolution and revenge
as a son of the human family?

If I'd been born into this gleaming-eyed
Tiger's raging world,
would I have survived to sire a son?
How different with my genes
would I have been?

◆　　◆　　◆

The shy eyes of Elizabeth Bishop
hiding in the pages of the magazine.
A child's eyes attacked by parasites
bred in the dammed and dying Nile.
The camera's eyes that peer into Andromeda
a billion years ago
and peek inside the DNA
that makes each one an "I."
The first eyes to detect light
that I am kin to
bobbing in primordial sea.

Elsewhere

while we sleep here, we are awake elsewhere
...in this way every man is two men
—Jorge Luis Borges

Letting go of my story
fitfully, another me
opens inside the sea.
Frogman drifting languidly
in indigo, riding the currents,
pulsing within realms
of moon jellies,
nearly fathoming strains
of dolphin conversation.
Only wishing not to witness
strife of teeth and tentacles,
not to see the white worms
trailing from anuses of cod
feeding on garbage,
no more bleached coral skeletons
and cracked conches on the floor.
Dimming vision drifting down
to tones of foreboding,
something roiling deeper,
groundswell of fear
of being swallowed by the sea.
Only there it is not drowning
but dying again into another,
finding sea legs on a deck
above the abyss in red weather.
It is rolling with pitch and yaw
between squalls of eels
that have to be shoveled into the sea.
Alive to stinging wind
and rope blisters,
fatigue driving the body down

to the drowsy noise and warmth
of the boilers, crawling inside
their incubating hum,
waking to familiar cravings and habits,
cheerful on the surface of dry land.

My Blue Coat

A man wearing my name
has just been released from prison.
Another has got it splayed

across the back of his jersey.
The ex-con has got a lazy way
of speaking, suave and convincing.

He asks if I will sponsor him
in the afterlife,
and the athlete is so sure-footed

and cocky, while on the dance floor
women step on my feet,
unwilling to follow my lead.

Or am I incapable of leading,
always *the baby of the family*,
not responsible for others,

for the racist remark
unleashed in my own dream.
Long ago I distanced myself

from nigger jokes, so how
did this foul-mouthed bigot
break into my head?

Or did he never escape?
The fool of a president
I disavow, but is he not comprised

of the same atoms as I,
as the sweet potato I'm intending to fry,
as the nineteen forty nine

Studebaker on parade?
Do I not feel the same fears
that fuel his demagoguery?

Are they not kindred to my worry
that a strand of my loose hair
will get into the hands of a voodoo man?

Or that cloners will use my spittle
to make a duplicate me?
What will they use for memories?

And I feel for my Turkish brother
whose body keeps fighting itself.
His doctors keep replacing joints.

Plastic wrists, ankles, hips,
knees like new.
At what point is he no longer

Ahmet, the boy I knew at seventeen?
When will I become no longer me,
that person given a certain name

born last of his brothers,
whose image of himself
keeps disassembling,

who dreams of fumbling through
a roomful of travelers' coats,
while from somewhere under the smothering

the word "nigger" is coupled with a curse.
He keeps unearthing blue coats,
but none that quite fits his mood.

None that covers my uncertainty.

Hats & Shoes

DNA in loose hairs
strewn by illiterate winds.
The follicle revealing

the chemical health of its owner,
or gleaned from a hat still warm
for voodoo,

the beggar wearing my lost beret
who is first to find the fallen man.
Ice, or clogged arteries

fumbling the foot, dumbing
the tongue thinking thanks
for the helping hand.

Thinking who could be
more self-conscious
than the brain-stricken man

unable to articulate,
who could have been I
crack-brained on black ice.

       ◆   ◆   ◆

In the dark the shoes by the beds
exhale.
Such heaviness released,

the extra steps trying to please,
the weight of comfort food,
sweat from tight situations.
Auschwitz' rooms of sorrowful shoes.

Imelda Marcos' hoard of shoes
barely broken in on plush floors.

One pair imprinted with the gait
of a lucky life, in a bag with old hats,
is given over to Goodwill.

◆　　◆　　◆

Icy wind of misfortune or witch's
spell, a slip on the staircase
of the cells' double-helix,

and I would've been the vagabond
rummaging through the bin
of used flip-flops, loafers, combat boots,

raising the scents of old owners
in an elevation of hosts.
Me fumbling for sandals to fit

my Christ-like self-image,
the sweat off my skin mingling
with the sweat of other homeless men

as an old fedora tumbles along the street
in the wind, its last owner's sweat
fast evaporating from the hatband.

Thumbstone

Walking dry creek bed recalling
the dream of wild-bearded Berryman
returned from the dead for a dinner party.
I'm the nurseryman in the yard,
Berryman is drunkenly flirting,
the same asshole he used to be,
though leaner and nearly bald.
The guests contend for his attention.
I want to trim his beard.

♦ ♦ ♦

Beneath me on the water's path
a thumb-sized stone.
It has me pick it up
and rub it over and over
between my finger and thumb.
Over and over, like memorizing
the 14th "Dream Song," becoming
its bored Henry, or papa Roethke's
Lost Son.

♦ ♦ ♦

Intent on rubbing it,
I stumble on rough rocks,
but keep my two digit grip,
kept Roethke's *Collected*
cradled in my hands
when my children needed nurture.

♦ ♦ ♦

Water moved this stone here
and smoothed it.
Sun-warmed, ruddy,
as if blood coursed inside,
now I'm its lifestream.
I imagine the chips
flaked from its side
reunited, and before that
the pieces fused to form
the man-sized slab
from which this thumbstone
broke away, and before that
the calving of the stratum
of grandfather stone.

        ♦   ♦   ♦

Would the mantle picture me
as a piece of Berryman
or chunk of Roethke rubble?
In whose dream are we tumbling
downstream, lost to our fathers,
found by our sons?
I keep rubbing it.

Narcissus at Christmas

Every year at Christmas my knee hurts
as I curse the crowds I have to wade through
to get her a gift of jewelry.

Every year she buys a forced narcissus
and places it so that its papery face
leans toward the glass and fumes.

Miraculous how it sprouts from a bed
of white rocks, how it exudes
the most cloysome scent of the season.

For a moment she frets
it's her menstruation she smells
instead of the breath

from this creamy bloom.
But soon at midnight mass
she'll become a little girl

among carols and candles
and altar boys swinging incense.
I won't disturb her reverie

to say her monthly visitor
is a miracle
beyond ten thousand Christmases.

She could dismiss such words
from me as a man,
but whose body is it

that aches and generates
the smell and the mess
if not the body of this blue Earth

facing the dark of the year,
Earth holding tight fists of tulips
in the underground cold.

Now the jeweler with the turban
like a great narcissus bulb,
so solicitous in my purchase

of her necklace, was a Sikh
for whom Christmas means brisk business.
Still, if it makes us partake

in rituals of generosity,
if I hide in a smile
the grimace of winter in my knee,

if I speak kindly to strangers
and breathe deeply
in the crush of Christmas traffic,

what might this body teach me?

Notes

"Gaudí's spires" in the title poem refers to the Temple Sagrada Família in Barcelona by Antoni Gaudí.

The epigraph in "Cancer" is from a lecture titled "Hodo Chameliontos" presented by Daniel Albright at the W. B. Yeats International Summer School in Sligo, Ireland. Among the artists and musicians referenced in the poem is Bob Marley, the father of reggae. The Spanish fascist dictator was turned into a grotesque polyp in Picasso's etching, *Dream and Lie of Franco*.

The passenger on the airliner in "Rooster" is reading a newspaper account of Air Egypt's October 31, 1999 Flight 990, said by investigators to have been deliberately brought down by a suicidal co-pilot.

"My Bad Twin"—"The Dark Enigma" is a repeated phrase from the early Taoist poet Po Chü-i, signifying the unfathomable mystery of creation. Leaves of the foxglove plant contain digitalis, a heart stimulant. The dishonest practice of feeding foxglove to worn-out horses in order to enhance their saleability is referenced in one of Po Chü-i's poems.

"Get Me God's Name"—The Jewish mystic Moses Maimonides states in *Guide of the Perplexed*, "...the description of God by means of negations is the correct description—a description that is not affected by an indulgence in facile language...With every increase in the negations regarding God, you come nearer to the apprehension of God." Chao Wen was a legendary lute player of ancient China. "What are the faces of your original parents?" (also referenced in "To Ann") is a Zen koan.

The ruins of Kayaköy and Hierapolis are in southwestern Anatolia, Turkey.

"Self-Portrait With Pets"—Differently-sized pupils is a symptom of Adies Pupil syndrome.

"The Invisible Man Dances With the Stripper" cites the name of Dostoevski's protagonist in *Crime and Punishment*.

In the poem, "Why Is The Body Politic?," Leyla Zana is the Kurdish member of the Turkish parliament imprisoned after making a plea for national unity in Kurdish to the parliament. Diribi Demissie is a member of the Oromo ethnic group of Ethiopia who was jailed for humanitarian fund-raising activities.

All of Me was composed by Gerald Marks with lyrics by Seymour Simons and popularized by Billie Holiday and Frank Sinatra.

In *"National Geographic,"* the Tigers are a revolutionary independence group.

The epigraph in "Elsewhere" is from Borges' "Tlön, Uqbar, Orbis Tersius," translated by James E. Irby.

This book of poetry has been published on acid free paper.
The type font is CG Omega.
♦   ♦   ♦

Printed in the United States
200105BV00014B/7-15/A